A Last Look

Robert Wells

A Last Look

A Last Look
published in the United Kingdom in 2016

by Mica Press
Leslie Bell, 47 Belle Vue Road, Wivenhoe, Colchester, Essex CO7 9LD
www.micapress.co.uk | books@micapress.co.uk

ISBN 978-1-869848-08-8

Copyright © Robert Wells 2016

The right of Robert Wells to be identified as the author of this work has been asserted by him in accordance with the
Copyright, Designs and Patents Act of 1988.
All rights reserved.

Acknowledgements:

'The Coin Cabinet' first appeared in *The Rialto,* 'Ionian' in *Agenda*, and 'Loggerhead' in the *Times Literary Supplement.*

Contents

'You are already leaving'	1
The Coin Cabinet	2
Ionian	5
Loggerhead	7
Lycian Sketches	8
The Garden	9
Winter Classroom, L'Aquila	13
The Smile	14
The Fall of Winston	15
Exmoor February	21
Time Out	22
In the Abruzzi	23
Group with Laptop	26
At Kirtlington	27

Notes

*With lively step
Or plodding resignation
I follow the track –
To the one destination.*

*What else remains to do
Or what more to say?
Everyman, young or old,
Is on his way.*

'You are already leaving...'

You are already leaving, the hills are closed
And this the goodbye after the last goodbye,

A last look back at the sprawling riverbed
Where what you had looked for stepped clear into view

– There that midday, at pause among the willows,
Embodied shade, drawn out of indistinctness

To form and colour, solidly visible,
Confirmed by air and water in its daydream.

The Coin Cabinet
(five trays)

1

Two calves' heads face-to-face, between them a tree.
A youth holding in a horse stung by a bee.
A parsley leaf. A corn-ear. A bunch of grapes.
An Amazon. A nymph whom a satyr rapes.
An opening rose. A swan flourishing its wings.
A prow. A tripod. A lyre with seven strings.
A crab, its pincers poised to repel attack.
A stag crouched with a clawing lion on its back.
A charioteer and team as they win the race
And take the prize. A spring, Arethusa's face
Freshly shaped in the water as it wells up.
Horse-tailed Silenos seated, tilting a cup.

2

A dolphin-rider above a curling sea.
A girl, half-stripped, in the branches of a tree,
Straddled by a bird, a bullock's head below.
Wrestlers grappling. An archer stringing a bow.
A double axe-head. A wheel. A vase. A lamp.
Thetis veiled, reclining on a hippocamp.
Herakles with the lion in his stranglehold,
Lovingly locked. A horned griffin guarding gold.
A turtle with spread flippers and studded shell
Paddling onward, aslant in the glassy swell.
Pan fagged with hunting, leant on a crag to rest
And turning to catch the breeze across his chest.

3

A gathered apple. Date-clusters on a palm.
Athena at war, her shield on her raised arm,
Spear poised. A brandished trident. A thunderbolt.
A cow scratching its muzzle. A prancing colt.
A ram. A tortoise. A bounding hare. A dove.
The sun-god's car, an eagle planing above.
A scarab-beetle. Two writhing snakes. A frog,
Softly defenceless. Unleashed, a hunting-dog
Seizing a fawn by the throat. Three seals at play.
A perched owl staring beside an olive-spray.
A feathered daimon. Gorgon baring her teeth.
A strutting cock. A pomegranate. A wreath.

4

A sea-eagle plucking its prey from the waves.
The head of a Maenad, wild-haired as she raves.
A Hydra. A Chimaera. A winged boar.
A soaring Pegasos. A squat Minotaur.
A Sphinx half-sitting, her slenderly curled haunch
A-quiver. Phoibos waving a laurel branch.
Hyakinthos kneeling, in his hand a flower.
Four horses at the gallop – one surge of power;
A snapped rein trailing, the turning-column down.
An old man with puckered face and balding crown.
Young Hermes gazing beneath his hat's broad brim
At the new shades that gather to follow him.

5

Two girls who carefully lift an amphora.
A discus-whirling boy. A crescent and star.
The head of Zeus, thick-bearded, intently calm.
Poseidon, a wave-worn cloak across his arm.
A sea-perch raising its spiky length of fin.
A close-fleshed tunny, tight in its oval skin,
Hauled from the water. Eight-armed, a cuttlefish.
A priestess by her altar, holding a dish.
A tensile vine. Dionysos, grave and slack,
Stretching comfortably on a donkey's back.
Demeter crowned with harvest, veil loosely furled
To greet her daughter, back from the underworld.

Ionian

O estuaries, anchorages

        that bay
where the fresh meeting the salt water
ran cold above it,
and the swimmer there
churning the levels together
started with his movement
– by some chemistry –
a precipitate,
clouding about his limbs.

O harbours, hinterlands

        a broken
sarcophagus on the foreshore;
a line of arches, weatherworn,
striding with vain purpose
into the wood
– too easily whetted
a taste for elegy,
the greeds and cruelties
long gone elsewhere.

O ragged coasts, rough capes

        the boat riding
offshore where no beach opened
– heave of water
against the abrupt stone,
a pine grove where cicadas
scratched their song so loud
by hot mid-morning
that the sound came
distinct across the surge.

O fellow-travelling creatures

          dolphins
within the prow's torn backwash
rising alongside,
embodiments of the wave
– suddenly, outside it
and ahead in varied play,
the propulsion without visible cause;
so, stationary-seeming
as if stamped in silver.

O evidences of passage

          ruts in rock,
a coin, a figurine,
potsherd litter, an amulet
pulled from riverbank-gravel
– less these leavings
than the journey retrieved and known,
sea true to its old epithets,
day measured by the sun
lifting and sinking.

LOGGERHEAD

Type of a courage to which the heart, intent
On its own journey, answers:
                          the sea-turtle,
Unwieldy solitary, tilted aslant,
Ferrying itself along through the green swell.

Lycian Sketches

1

Stone tombs like hold-alls
abandoned on a station platform,

in the shade an old sailor
come back to his own village;

the rock-ridge necropolis arid
above a red-soiled valley

where corn in circles
is being threshed and winnowed.

2

Marshbound waters, silted havens,
sites quick with traffic
turned to enclaves of fever:

O pastoral by default!

– a quayside granary, its rugged facade
and foursquare walls
become a picturesque item,
glimpsed unreachably
across a vista of reeds.

The Garden
i.m. Brenda Dowson

What remains of those forays
when, girlish as ever,
you'd set off in your light
blue sunhat, with brisk light tread –
gloves, trowel, secateurs
and cigarettes in hand,
as ever exclaiming
at how late you'd left it,

O my godfathers
– sure-footed on the mule-track
despite your seventy,
your eighty years... to the same
vacant stretch of meadow,
your garden? It never took shape!
A few untended roses
and straggling oleanders

still make a doubtful show
between the olives and vines,
with – here and there – the flourish
of some staunch denizen
returning, spring by spring,
to the nook you found for it
among scabius and chicory
one bygone afternoon.

What became of that effort,
those hours, that fantasy
which drew you into its trance,
conjuring time and to spare
for the piecemeal task
while you lived for the day
imagined, imaginary
when all would coalesce?

How was it I didn't see
that those rapt intervals
enacted a kind of dare:
coolly, continuously,
you were flouting an opponent,
who must surely be around,
impalpable stalker,
somewhere just out of range?

Here, under long grass,
the little travertine plaque
marks with initials and dates
where your expatriate ashes
were emptied illegally out,
the urn flown home, its customs
paperwork in order –
containing household cinders:

your wish, our subterfuge!
No cemetery should have you,
least of all the dapper
precinct in silhouette
(if ever from your side
of the valley you glanced across)
on the slope above the village,
squared off with cypresses.

For death you had no time.
You carried yourself proudly
as if to hold it away
by the sheer dismissive force
of your prejudice, that stare
practised in youth to guard
a beauty which turned heads,
those put-downs you reserved

for some awkward hanger-on
sent packing: 'not exactly
a ball of fire', or 'actually
I feel sorry for him'. So
you'd bend to your transplanted
orchids, your slips and seedlings
intently, with much to do,
disdaining interruption.

Death had to come in secret
(you would have refused to allow,
even had you suspected it,
that you had been accosted):
a tick, a horse-fly bite,
some trivial annoyance
to be brushed off or ignored;
the sequelae unremarked

through blankly ensuing days
of misidentified fever,
which you sought to scare away
with the rattle of the pill-box;
no inkling till, ten minutes
before the end, a felt
shift, and the words you left
till last, 'I think I'm dying'.

How vulnerably defiant
you were out on that open
hillside, or later in the high-walled
derelict *vasca* behind
the mill, your 'watergarden'
(the name was almost enough):
your last least-realized dream,
the one most real to you.

Where the stream fans idly
through willowherb and briar,
your stepping-stones displaced
under gravel or grassy mud –
no trace now of the cherished
vision which kept you busy,
no remnant visible
of all your interventions,

except... except for this clump
of dark bamboos, their smoky
stems asway, their fibrous
leaves uneasily sighing
as they brush against one another
in graceful discontent
– a thriving rarity
fetched here and planted by you.

Your emblem, your self unselved! –
as if, evasive still
even in the desperate moment,
you had, as your one recourse
to baffle the pursuit,
abruptly shed your body
and fled into the bamboo
and transformed were still here.

Winter Classroom, L'Aquila

My truant pupils
come in, brown from skiing,
matter-of-factly unapologetic
(the low sky sullen again
after dry fine days).

They bring an absence with them
neither room nor hour
nor my contrived insistences
dispel.
      Wide-eyed, spaced-out,
for them first things are happening
and still to happen
on the drifted blankness of the slopes,

the track they leave there only incidentally
their own, a gliding into distance,
body continuous
with sun and snow.

The Smile

What I believe in is that open face.
Where that clear smile is to be found I go
Gratefully, as to a spring:
                               its pulsing flow
In some deserted and long-looked-for place.

The Fall of Winston
– *an Exmoor fable*

He was the household favourite,
a handsome border collie,
two years old (his pedigree
immaculate), with a glossy
coat, its cream-and-tan
luxuriantly flouncing
as he pranced and leapt among us,
or streaming out as he raced;

the paragon at once
of beauty and good-nature,
petted and friendly, yet
preserving a seductive
aloofness. Who could fail
to be flattered by attentions
from such a creature, himself
the centre of attention?

A quarter trained perhaps
(the rest, so ran the hopeful
refrain, would come in time),
he sat beside his master
in the Land Rover, a companion,
the dog from the great house,
and would spring out with a flourish,
momentarily at heel,

when, in the lambing season,
his master toured the farms
and stayed to share the labour.
So, when the fields were walked
last thing in the evening
to ensure that the young lambs
were with their dams, the doubles
together, properly paired,

Winston had only to appear
in a field-corner, by the gate,
like a transfigured fox,
to make the ewes look up
alarmed and, suddenly reminded,
look about them for their young.
The pairing-off at dusk
went smoothly. He was good for that.

But with other tasks, wherever
steadiness or accurate
obedience were called for,
he was something of a joke.
The tenants and the farm-hands
looked on, and did not smile,
fearing, where they saw a weakness,
that the moor might find it out.

His master would send Winston
to run with the working dogs;
it seemed he couldn't or wouldn't
learn from them. They knew
to a T what was required,
what was permitted. Living
by rule in little packs,
competing among themselves,

they ignored him, as a nuisance
sometimes in their way.
Fawning, observant, instantly
reactive, neither beautiful
nor ugly, they looked for commands
where he would look for favours
– an exception would at least
be made for any failure.

Winston had his kennel
at the back of the great house
by the kitchen door (and dined there
on choicest scraps). At night
he was shut out – no need
to chain him. Where would he go,
secluded as the house was
under steep wood-hung coombs?

So too by day, off duty,
he had the run of the garden,
its terraced lawns, its rosebeds,
on a shelf above sheer cliffs.
The farms were a mile away
or further, up on the moor,
over the brow of the seaward
escarpment, looking inland.

As he circuited the garden
Winston, briskly high-stepping,
had worn a path in the lawn.
A clear line athwart the even
expanse and encompassing
the house, it surely signalled
that he belonged, had his part
– superfluous as that might be –

in the routine of the place.
It was noted with affection
from the dining-room, the parlour,
from the library bay-window:
there it was, Winston's track,
and there he was, too, rounding
a corner, combed by the breeze,
on his swift absorbed patrol.

Word came from the farms one day:
a dog had been worrying sheep
in the top fields. Pregnant ewes
had been found bloodied and harried
on several mornings. A stray dog
(our thoughts fixed angrily
on the outcast interloper).
A watch would be kept. Word came

that the dog resembled Winston,
that it was Winston. The truth
broke by degrees, eked out
with tact, on successive days...
Hill-farmers' eyes don't make
mistakes, not in such matters:
Winston's night-wandering
stood confirmed. As for the proof

– though it only served to clinch
the fact already known –
his mouth was opened, his teeth
examined. There, at the back,
around the base of his molars,
lay twisted in, tell-tale,
a deposit of encrusting
grey-white strands of fleece.

Winston was a dead dog
from that moment. Nothing was said.
I, deaf to the unspoken,
supposed he would be confined
merely – as he was that night.
A way out would be devised
no doubt, some practical
adjustment made... Next morning,

neither sadly nor angrily
– it was all that remained to do,
a last formality –
his master unchained Winston
and drove him to the vet
(the favourite's privilege
to be 'put down' – a farm-dog
would have been shot out of hand).

There could be no goodbyes
of course – an obscenity
to allow him back among us.
The moor held, unforgiving,
to its tried and rigid law:
such a dog is incorrigible,
cannot be trusted, the taste
once got is never forgotten...

Proscription without appeal!
I learnt of it afterwards,
his master's quiet aside
that evening in the kitchen,
the table cleared: Winston
in the Roman phrase, 'had lived'.
That was all. And no one
mentioned him again.

*

Years later, revisiting
the house, I willed myself
to try his name, and asked
(my question half-concealed
amid other reminiscence)
what they, his master's son
– a child then – and his master
recalled of the incident.

No response. For his master
the name, the dog, the event
had gone clean out of mind.
The son could just remember
that there had been such a dog
but nothing of what happened.
For me alone then – unless
he figures, as a caution,

in a farm-hand's anecdote –
he remains a presence still.
Whenever 'cruel necessity'
is invoked, or a 'criminal'
obsession is brought to light,
or event throws into relief
our conditional affections,
Winston bounds into view

with that lordly vitality
which could not plead for him
– as if he had just returned
through coombs seaming the hills
from a savage secret foray,
having found his long way up,
pricked on by unaccommodated
instinct, to the dark top fields.

Exmoor February

1

An early lambing:
life after slippery life
hauled into cold air.

2

In the yard-corner
a heap of carcasses, cleared
weekly by the Hunt.

3

Birth and death crowding
into the days: far frontiers
nearer, more exact.

4

A world's width enclosed
by fields named and known: Breakneck,
Middlemead, the Plat.

Time Out

He wakes each morning
blurred by an energy
without aim or concentration

– the soft wishes
of a life become all wish.

His thoughts are of pools, sun-shafts,
dew-wet glades.

★

A plank-bridge above a stream,
the grain of the wood
worn clear by weather;
stopped there

he watches, not the water's flow
but how the light
vibrates along it

in a ceaseless dazzling wave.

In the Abruzzi

The incident discovers its meaning now –
At least, such sense as can be attributed
After forty years...
               A sunlit city square,
Low houses shuttered against the afternoon,
A fountain trickling into its bowl, a church,
Locked, the stone frontage darkly corrugated,
Rough walls and basalt pavement giving back heat.

On the further side, parked in a strip of shade,
Not seen at first, a bus – a blue *corriera*
Of the always-superannuated kind
That serves the mountain villages, and tumbles
The postbag out together with passengers;
Picks up, sets down at unnamed halts and by-ways,
Its horn listened out for along hairpin roads.

The driver not yet arrived, the little crowd
It brought to town this morning gathers by it –
Country people with their bundles and baskets,
Pleased to linger and gossip, their errands done.

At the near corner stands a kiosk, displaying
Newspapers, lottery tickets, cigarettes,
Biscuits and sweets, a carton or two of fruit.
Some of the passengers press round the counter,
Reaching over each other excitedly
To make last-minute purchases. I stop too
For some small item.
                  Shut in my own concerns,
I hardly notice the stir in front of me
Until it takes a more particular form:
A thickset elderly man in a black hat,
Dark coat and tieless shirt buttoned at the neck –
A *contadino*'s garb – begins to bargain
For a large bunch of bananas, which (a sum
Settled upon after much fine deployment

Of rhetoric) he clumsily endeavours
(Clutching a canvas umbrella tight beneath
One elbow) to manoeuvre into his bag,
Its zip catching, its imitation leather
Stiff and cracked.
                Suddenly, exuberantly,
He swings about to face me (having put down
The bananas on the counter) and holds out
The empty bag by the handles: 'Tienilo,
Che sei giovane!' He looks me up and down –
A short pause – fixes his eyes on mine, and adds
In a voice both mocking and tenderly meant,
The words clear and deliberate as his stare,
'Figlio del biondo Apollo, fratello
Delle Muse'.
            Then, as if rallying me
At my surprise and somehow disappointed
In his challenge, 'Ma sei educato, eh?'

Inwardly delighted, inwardly reproached,
I have no come-back. I hold the bag as asked
While he transfers the bananas; taking it
He thanks me curtly, turns, strolls off to the bus –
Now opened by the driver – and climbs aboard,
Disappearing at once among the others.

Nonplussed I make my purchase, stand there and watch
As the rackety vehicle pulls slowly
Round the fountain-basin and out of the square,
Carrying him, unplaceable as he seems,
Seer or showman, back to where he came from.

> *Sons of blonde Apollo, the Muses' brother,*
> *Are two-a-penny. What makes the difference*
> *Is how each lives up to the salutation*
> *In the long sequel.*
>   *As in the first instant,*
> *Touched by the occasion, unequal to it?*

Many times I have imagined that village,
The bus finding its way by an unknown road
To a lost canton, happily off the map,
Where an old rite and shrine remain undamaged
Perhaps, as the perennial fable recounts;
Where the angst and inhibition clouding youth,
Blinding it to its luck, are lifted away,
The hidden godhead recognized and challenged.

GROUP WITH LAPTOP

Like Poussin's shepherds confronted by the stone
Sarcophagus with its graven apophthegm
(Propped there discreetly, a skull stares back at them;
The rivergod tilts his urn; their girl looks on
Breast bared, her loose drape gathered about her thigh;
An elegiac glint touches leaves and clouds –
While the foremost of them leans to test the words
With unbelieving finger and startled eye):

These also, in the energy of their prime
Surprised and challenged, taking their turn in time
As if no others had lived and died, now press
Forward raptly, shepherds as they might have been,
To spell out the message printed on the screen:
'I too was a receiver of consciousness'.

At Kirtlington

I came here to search for fossils.
                              Even and odd,
Matching lamellibranch, beaked brachiopod,
Slipped from the limestone shelf where they lay packed
At the tap of my hammer – name and fact
Declaring themselves frankly in my open palm,
Newly discovered shapes.
                              The quarry, calm
As an empty amphitheatre, lay around
Wide-floored, vast in its space and air: a ground
Where I first sensed how it might be to accept
What, undeclared, must stay mere secret kept
For its own sake, locked in a brittle shelf –

So found I was less a stranger to myself.

Notes

'The Coin Cabinet'

I love Greek coins, and cannot afford to collect them. This then is my virtual collection. My subject is the way in which the coins of each city (and there are a myriad cities) sum up a particular place and the life of a place in a chosen image, an instance of concentrated design. Put together, the many images represent the variousness of a world – that world from which, at the close of the fourth stanza, Hermes escorts the recent dead, and to which Persephone returns at the close of the fifth. It is my fancy that the exact syllable-count stands for the exactness of the stamped design, while the irregular rhythms stand for the coins' other irregularities of shape. For some information and phrasing I am indebted to *Ancient Greek Coins* by G. K. Jenkins (Barrie & Jenkins, 1972).

'Loggerhead'

I was thinking of seventeenth-century emblem poems. But the turtle is a real one, seen off the island of Melos some forty years ago.

'Group with Laptop'

The painting is the one in the Devonshire Collection at Chatsworth, not Poussin's later treatment of the 'Et in Arcadia Ego' theme in the Louvre.

'At Kirtlington'

Lamellibranch and brachiopod are two kinds of bivalve mollusc, the halves of the shell of the lamellibranch meeting evenly at the hinge, while in the brachiopod one half comes to a point which reaches over the other. The *ch* in both words is hard.

www.ingramcontent.com/pod-product-compliance
Lightning Source LLC
Chambersburg PA
CBHW042131100526
44587CB00026B/4254